NEW UNITED LEGEND
A Tribute to David Beckham

NEW UNITED LEGEND
A TRIBUTE TO DAVID BECKHAM

Bobby Blake

MAINSTREAM
PUBLISHING

EDINBURGH AND LONDON

First published in Great Britain in 1997 by
MAINSTREAM PUBLISHING COMPANY (EDINBURGH) LIMITED
7 Albany Street
Edinburgh EH1 3UG

ISBN 1 84018 009 9

A catalogue record for this book is available from the British Library

Designed by Ian McPherson

Printed and bound in Great Britain by The Bath Press Colourbooks, Glasgow

Contents

1   **Goal Of the Century**   7

2   **The Road to United**   13

3   **Fergie's Flegdlings**   18

4   **Double Vision**   30

5   **Spends and Spice Girls**   42

6   **England's Dreaming**   53

Goal of the Century

United were already 2–0 up and looked to have the game won when Brian McClair stroked a simple pass with the outside of his boot up to the young number 10 on the right.

Having thrown most of their men forward in a desperate attempt to get a goal, now Wimbledon were streaming back to intercept the sudden counter-attack. Even goalkeeper Neil Sullivan found himself backpedalling from the edge of his penalty area, where he had been perched while Wimbledon attacked, urging his team on.

But it was already too late. As he reached the halfway line, the young United number 10 swung his right foot under the ball and lifted it high into the Selhurst Park sky.

Three seconds later, it landed smack into the back of the Wimbledon net, Neil Sullivan left grasping at thin air as the United supporters behind the goal leapt to their feet and roared their approval in a strange mixture of delight and disbelief.

"Oh! That it is absolutely phenomenal!" cried *Match Of The Day* commentator John Motson, and for once he wasn't exaggerating. "David Beckham — surely an England player of the future — scores a goal that will be talked about and replayed for years!"

Dead right, Motty. It was August 17, the opening day of the 1996–7 season, and with that one, incredible 57-yard shot, David Beckham, Manchester United's latest and perhaps greatest young discovery, had already scored what would surely be the Goal of the Season.

Some pundits went even further and called it Goal of the Century — though not even Beckham's footie-mad dad, Ted, would go that far. One thing everybody agreed on, at the tender age of just 21 years and three months, Becks, as his friends and team-mates call him, had scored the kind of wonder-goal that not even the Great Cantona himself had ever managed.

Certainly, the closest modern day comparisons would be Pele's failed attempt from just inside the halfway line for Brazil against Czechoslovakia in the World Cup in Mexico, 1970, and Nayim's spectacular, long-range effort for Real Zaragoza against Arsenal in the dying seconds of the European Cup Winners Cup final, in 1995. But Pele missed (just) and Nayim was the first to admit afterwards that his goal had been massively mis-hit and was more like fluke of the century!

When Becks hit the ball from the halfway line against Wimbledon, he knew exactly what he was doing; he had seen Sullivan off his line and fully intended to have a shot on goal. That he pulled it off and scored says as much about his fierce ambition as it does the abundant talent of United's newest and brightest young star.

Since then, the phrase 'done a Beckham' has passed into every day usage for footie fans up and down the country, any long range shot on goal, be it in the playground or on the hallowed turf of Wembley, qualifying for the accolade.

As modest off the field as he is supremely gifted on it, Becks himself admits the goal against Wimbledon will probably be the greatest he ever scores (unless of course he scores one just like it for England in the World Cup final!).

"Not just because it was unique," he says, "but the fact it came on the opening day of the season made it more special. I have seen replays of the goal, but if I'm honest, you could try that shot a hundred times and it would never come off."

He says he remembers receiving the pass from McClair, seeing the Wimbledon goal up ahead and just thinking he should bash the ball into it as though it were in front of him, not halfway up a football pitch.

"We already had the game won at 2–0 and when I received the ball inside my own half I spotted Neil Sullivan off his line and thought, 'Why not, let's have a go!'. It's one of those goals that I will look back on in a few years time and think, 'Did I really do that?'"

Becks had scored for United in the opening game of the season the previous year as well, bagging a second-half consolation as United went down 3–1 at Aston Villa. An occasion which prompted former Liverpool and Scotland defender, and now *Match Of The Day* pundit, Alan Hansen's famous quote: "You can't win anything with kids."

They were words, of course, that Hansen was later forced to cut into small pieces and swallow, but understandable, perhaps, at the time. Hansen was merely giving expression to a feeling that many United supporters themselves shared — that Alex Ferguson had acted too quickly in selling off established international stars like Andrei Kanchelskis, Mark Hughes and Paul Ince and putting his faith in a group of admittedly talented but largely inexperienced young-sters, whose average age was then just 20.

Back then, Becks was just another of the flash young guns Manchester United had limbering up; one of a highly promising generation of United youth-team graduates, including Nicky Butt, Paul Scholes and Gary and Philip Neville, whom the press had dubbed 'Fergie's Fledglings'.

Now, two seasons later, in which he has helped United to their second Premier League and FA Cup Double in two

---

GOAL OF THE CENTURY: BECKHAM'S MIRACLE!

DENIS IRWIN
"There have been quite a few good goals this season, but that one by Becks against Wimbledon still stands out. He's got his own personal collection of great goals, but that one's slightly different to the rest."

GEORGE BEST
(Speaking before David's strike...)
"To lob the goalkeeper from inside your own half must be possible. Someone, some day, will do it, but not, I fear, any British player. They haven't got the footballing intelligence to try it."

ERIC HARRISON (MAN UTD YOUTH TEAM COACH)
"David has always been a very talented player, and I'm not just jumping on the bandwagon — I've been singing his praises for a couple of years now. Take his goal at Wimbledon. Initially, it surprised me, but I remembered the times he tried it for the Youth team. Given his long-range shooting and passing, I shouldn't have really been surprised."

TED BECKHAM (DAVID'S FATHER)
"What meant most to David was Cantona shaking his hand after the game and saying, 'Beautiful goal, David'."

The young Becks in full flow for United

Beckham celebrates in fine style. It's become a familiar sight for the United faithful

years, their fourth Premiership title in five years and the semi-final of the European Champions League (their best showing in the competition since 1969 and the glory days of Sir Matt Busby's classic Best-Law-Charlton side), he has become an established England international, a heart-throb to millions of teenage girls, a hero to as many more football-mad boys, and the name David Beckham is known throughout the world as one of the most exciting young stars of the English Premiership.

This book tells the story of the phenomenal rise to fame and glory of the 'kid' they call the new Bobby Charlton, the new Glenn Hoddle and the new Paul Gascoigne all rolled into one.

This book tells the story of a 16-year-old schoolboy who nervously left behind the family home in Leytonstone, East London, to set off for the bright lights of Old Trafford and Manchester, and who hasn't looked back since.

It tells the story of the most exciting and gifted player to wear the red No.10 shirt in a Manchester United side since Mark 'The Legend' Hughes scored his final goal in the famous red and white.

This book tells the story of David Beckham.

Becks powers past
Blackburn's
Stuart Ripley

David may have burst onto the Old Trafford scene, but it was a long road to the top

The Road to United

While Kevin Keegan tried to buy the Premiership title with the £15 million he persuaded Newcastle to pay Blackburn for Alan Shearer, Alex Ferguson raised more eyebrows with his sales than his acquisitions.

To the shock and dismay of many, a year before Fergie had off-loaded Hughes, Ince and Kanchelskis, only abating the wrath of the fans (some of whom actually wrote to the club demanding his resignation!) when he then went on to lead United to their second League and Cup Double in two years.

Striker Ole Gunnar Solskjaer and defender Ronny Johnsen arrived that summer from Norway, quickly followed by the attacking midfielder Karel Poborsky, and Jordi Cruyff from Barcelona.

But only Solskjaer and Johnsen would go on to claim a regular place in the first-team, crowded out by the products of United's superb youth scheme; boys Fergie had helped turn into men, moulding an outstanding crop of FA Youth Cup-winning talent.

Defenders like Gary and Philip Neville, who have grown into their roles so well they would both graduate into the England first-team. Once, they found themselves in the strange position of Gary being first choice at right-back for Terry Venables' England, while Philip was Alex Ferguson's first choice for Manchester United!

Striker Paul Scholes, nicknamed 'Goalsey Scholesy' after knocking in 25 goals in 25 matches for the Youth A-team when he first joined the club as a trainee in 1991, is now seen by many as the long-term replacement for Cantona, and has also become a recent recruit to Glenn Hoddle's England squad.

And the fiery midfielder, Nicky Butt, now Roy Keane's combative midfield partner, has proved such an able replacement for Paul 'The Guv'nor' Ince that he, too, has now forced his way into the full England squad.

But none has been as immediately dazzling as the emergence of United's most brilliant and exciting young player of the Nineties, David Beckham.

"It's a special young player that can play in the first team," says Fergie. "It's the temperament, as well as the ability." And Becks is blissfully blessed with both.

David Robert Joseph Beckham was born in Leytonstone, East London, on May 2, 1975. These days, at six-foot in his socks and weighing just 11st 2lb, he is lean, fast and powerful, capable of running at defences, and able to pass and shoot from literally any angle.

But growing up kicking a ball around with his mates on the streets of London's grimy East End, Becks was just another skinny kid who was good at dribbling. Always one of the first to be picked to play, whether it was in the playground or on the sports field, it was obvious from the word go that Becks was 'useful' with a ball at his feet.

As a junior school pupil, the young Beckham already played in the school side the year above his own, and for a local club side called Ridgeway Rovers, where he was to score 101 goals in 115 games over a three-year undefeated run. He remembers chipping the goalie from 20-yards — a phenomenal shot at that age; the schoolboy equivalent of what he would do against Wimbledon ten years later.

He was, he says, always a Manchester United supporter, drawn to the allure of the club by his father Ted's unbridled love of all things Red. They still joke in the Beckham household about who was the most excited when Becks actually ended up signing to United: David or his dad.

Becks says his father's support and encouragement were important ingredients in his desire to succeed at Old Trafford. Ted Beckham has regularly followed his son to games since he was in the youth side, and these days you will find him at most of United's first-team matches, whether David is playing or not.

And yet, it was nearly all so different. In fact, if the fates had been just a fraction off, David Beckham might be known today as Tottenham Hotspur's star young player. Enthusiastically recommended to the club by a scout after witnessing another one of his goal-scoring outings for Ridgeway Rovers, Beckham was invited to train at Spurs, in January 1986.

Becks trained twice a week with the youth teams and reserves at White Hart Lane. But even then, he would turn

THE BECKS FILES: THE LOWDOWN ON DAVID

BORN: Leytonstone, London, May 2, 1975
HEIGHT: 6' 0
WEIGHT: 11st. 2lb
POSITION: Midfield
Signed as a trainee at Manchester United: July 1991.
Signed full professional forms at Manchester United: January 1993.

FIRST TEAM DEBUT
Came on as sub, away to Brighton, 2nd Round Coca Cola Cup, September 23, 1992. Full First Team Debut: away to Port Vale, 2nd Round Coca-Cola Cup, September 21, 1994.

PREMIERSHIP DEBUT
Home to Leeds United, April 2, 1995.

FIRST GOAL
Home to Galatasaray, December 7, 1994.

MORE FIRSTS
First Premiership goal; away to Aston Villa, August 19, 1995.
England Under-21 Debut; against Brazil, June 1995.
First time of captaining his country at representative level; Under-21 tournament, Toulon, France, May 1996.

CAPS, AWARDS AND STATS
Away to Moldova, World Cup qualifier, September 1, 1996
Voted Sky TV's Young Player of the Year; January 1997
Voted Young Player Of The Year by the Professional Footballers Association: April 1997.
(Incredibly, David also came second in the actual Player Of The Year category, beaten only by Alan Shearer!)
Goals and first-team games for United: 1994–5 — four games, no goals; 1995–6 — 39 games, 8 goals; 1996–7, 41 games, 9 goals.

Beckham in the white of England. He almost wore the white of Tottenham Hotspur, too!

up wearing his red Manchester United kit. "I took a lot of stick for that," he recalled with a smile years later. "But I didn't care, I loved United."

But why hadn't he stayed at Tottenham? How did a club, normally so astute in judging the potential of young players (their youth teams rivalling United's own in recent years for FA Youth Cup honours), let such a prodigious talent as the young David Beckham slip through its fingers?

Fittingly, it was an intervention by the United player Becks would later be most compared to, Sir Bobby Charlton, that first took the teenage Beckham to Old Trafford, when he was encouraged to enrol in a Sir Bobby Charlton Soccer School course — an association that led to the 12-year-old David once leading United out as mascot.

At the end of the day, it was down to the personal touch. Terry Venables, usually renowned for his dealings with younger players, was managing Tottenham at the time, but Becks only got to meet the future England coach once while he was there.

"That doesn't exactly inspire you to join the club," says Becks now. "And United were the friendliest club I went to and that is what swayed me the most. Alex Ferguson was brilliant with me."

Fergie provided a fatherly figure for all his young players; he understood how important it was to protect them from the wayward outside influences that have been the undoing of more than one promising young career over the years.

"It's a commitment to them and their parents," says Fergie. "They leave home in the morning and we look after them during the day and I want to make sure they go home the same person."

And so it was that the 16-year-old David Beckham moved up to Manchester, in the summer of 1991, where he was formally signed as a Manchester United trainee on July 8. Enrolled into United's own School of Excellence, he would receive extensive tactical and fitness training, and get the opportunity to try and make his name in the Youth A and B teams.

Leaving his family and friends behind in London for the strange new sights of Manchester was not the easiest thing he had ever done, Becks admits now. But it was a drastic change of scene that proved helpful in unexpected ways. Not being able to hang out with all his old school mates meant it wasn't so easy to be dragged into going out at night to pubs and clubs, stuff that would detract from his burgeoning career as a full-time footballer.

And at Old Trafford, the club was so big and the stars that played for it so great, there was no chance of slacking or thinking that you knew it all. Becks had always been one of the best players in any side he'd been in since he was seven. Now he found himself surrounded by other lads just

"And for my next trick..." Becks gets loosened up

Beckham in European action against Rapid Vienna

as talented, just as desperate for a chance to prove themselves. For the first time in his life, Becks was learning to fight for his place in the team.

"At United, the kids [like Beckham] are hungry for success — that's just how it is," says Gary Pallister. "Here you're not just playing against other teams but against people coming through at the club. You have to earn your place, otherwise you're out of the team. And once you've been at Old Trafford, there's only one place you're going and that's down." It kept you humble; kept you focussed. As a trainee apprentice, Becks would be one of the first at the training ground every morning, cleaning boots and sweeping out the floors.

"When you first arrive at Man United, you're scared of just about everything," says Gary Neville, who was signed at the same time as Becks. For some, it was an angst-ridden nightmare; for others, like Becks, it was a dream come true.

"It is a dream to play here," says Philip Neville, who made the full England squad at 19. "Walking out of the tunnel is amazing. At about 2.55 pm on a Saturday it's the biggest noise I've ever heard — louder than Wembley."

"You just have to look at the club's record," says Ole Gunnar Solskjaer, just a year older than Becks. "Everything about the club is huge. Think of the players who have played here: Bobby Charlton, George Best, the Busby Babes. Everyone wants to play here."

"I gave up a lot when I was younger," says Becks. "Going out with the lads, going to parties and discos, leaving my family to come up to Manchester. It was what I wanted though, so I made my choices."

Choices that had soon paid off handsomely. In his first season playing for United's A-team, they won the 1992 FA Youth Cup; the following year, they were runners-up — 12 months in which Becks had also made his first team debut for United, against Brighton in the Coca-Cola Cup, in September 1992, and had played as an England Under-21 international, winning caps against France, Switzerland, Spain and Denmark.

But by then he was on a roller-coaster ride that would gradually grow bigger and faster and more hypnotic than either Becks or Fergie or the most fervent United fans could ever have dreamed possible.

Fergie's Fledglings

avid Beckham signed full professional forms for Manchester United on January 23, 1993. He was given a four-year contract and became part of an intake that would not only come to dominate the United first team but would all graduate within the next few years into the full England side.

Some would have found the competition for first-team places at Old Trafford daunting, but Becks himself says he thrived on being surrounded by the brightest and the best, knowing he had to produce the goods if he wanted to become an established first-team player.

What Becks brought to the party were his pace (his sprint-partner at The Cliff, the club's training ground,

is Ryan Giggs, making Becks one of the two fastest runners in the side), his passing (equally accurate over four yards or 40), his shooting (ask Neil Sullivan), and his passion (bred into him by his father).

When you try and imagine how much it would now cost another team to buy the likes of Beckham, Giggs, Butt, Scholes, and the Nevilles, it's clear that Alex Ferguson's youth policy has saved Manchester United tens of millions of pounds over the years. As a result, these days Fergie is hailed as a genius.

But his work behind the scenes at Old Trafford wasn't always so universally appreciated. It took time for the seeds of success to grow, and it might be said that the

Lee Sharpe, Roy Keane
and a short-haired
Becks celebrate

Beckham quickly found out you had to fight for things at United

story of David Beckham is also the story of how Fergie restored to Old Trafford the same flourishing youth policy that had provided the club with the legendary 'Busby Babes' back in the Fifties.

Matt Busby's celebrated youth policy — "my Golden Apples," he called them — and his astute use of the club's cheque-book combined to win United the League Championship three times in the Fifties. With most of the side barely out of their teens, like now, they were the most skilful and glamorous team in the country.

When Busby and the directors of the club defied the powers that be in the English League — who originally disapproved of the idea — to become the first British team to enter the European Cup, in 1957, they seemed bound for glory.

The first Golden Age in the history of Manchester United, it was cut tragically short when eight members of the Busby Babes were killed in February 1958, when their plane crashed on take-off from Munich airport, returning from a European Cup fixture against Red Star Belgrade. Amongst the dead was their legendary 21-year-old captain and England international, Duncan Edwards, still considered by those who remember him as potentially the greatest player the club have ever produced.

Who knows what glories that team might have achieved had they lived long enough to reach their dizzy peak. They would almost certainly have run away with their fourth Division One Championship, and may even have completed the club's first historic Double, as they had also qualified again for the final of the FA Cup.

In the event, with a team patched together from hastily purchased replacements and willing reserves, United understandably failed to win either trophy that year. Indeed, it was another five years before United next won anything — a 3–1 victory over Leicester City in the final

Wembley to win the 1968 European Cup, for which Busby was knighted.

But it took all his remaining strength to do so and without Busby's ferocious energy to support it, the youth-structure that had been the club's pride and joy in the Fifties slowly disintegrated, and with it, the United fans' dreams of reclaiming the glory they had known under his leadership.

When Alex Ferguson arrived at Old Trafford in November 1986, he discovered a club that was not so much a sleeping giant as completely comatose. The five managers that had come and gone since Sir Matt had retired in 1971, had won the FA Cup three times and the Charity Shield twice, but had never come close to winning the League title for the club. One, Tommy Docherty, even took them down to the old Division Two for a season, though they did win the Division Two Championship the following year to bring them straight back up.

These were the grey, listless years of Manchester United, the long, consistent run of domestic and European Championships their deadliest rivals, Liverpool, accumulated in the Seventies and Eighties only serving to highlight United's own paucity of achievements throughout the same period.

Born in Govan, a small shipyard community in the west of Scotland, in 1941, Alex Ferguson was a manager very much in the image of Sir Matt himself. The motto that used to hang above the gates of the now closed Govan shipyard — 'Nihil Sine Labour' (nothing without work) — now sits proudly on the wall of Fergie's Manchester United office, reflecting a deep pride in his working class, Calvinist roots.

As a player, Fergie was an honest and reliable striker whose career took him up and down the Scottish Leagues with Queens Park, St Johnstone, Dunfermline,

Fergie's Fledglings were the new 'Babes'...

of the 1963 FA Cup that deflected attention away from the fact that the team had been fighting against relegation all season.

As history shows, Busby, who himself had barely survived the crash, would eventually build a new, Championship-winning Manchester United side in the Sixties around the cornerstones of Bobby Charlton (an original Busby Babe and fellow crash-survivor), George Best (the most exciting talent, after Duncan Edwards, that Busby ever unearthed), and Denis Law (his most glamorous signing). And of course, we all know that he went on to land United the ultimate prize of all, beating Benfica 4–1 after extra-time at

Glasgow Rangers, Falkirk, Ayr and, finally, lowly East Stirling, where his managerial career began as player-coach, in 1974.

Soon poached by St Mirren, Fergie first made a name for himself as a manager to be reckoned with when he steered the side to the Scottish First Division Championship in 1976–7, winning them promotion for the first time to the Scottish Premiership.

The big boys began to take notice and the following summer a move was made to take Ferguson to Aberdeen. The next decade saw Fergie lead his Pittodrie side to an unprecedented period of success in the club's history: three Scottish Premiership Championships, four Scottish

Beckham got an extra buzz out of scoring this one — the congratulations of his hero Eric Cantona...

Cup victories (including the League and Cup Double in 1984), and the European Cup Winners' Cup, in 1983.

When Aberdeen won their first Scottish Premiership under Fergie in 1980, they became the first team other than Rangers or Celtic to do so for 15 years. More remarkable, they were able to break the Old Firm's stranglehold on Scottish football by giving free reign to some of the finest young talent to come out of Scotland for years.

However, it was also at Aberdeen that Fergie learned to his cost what happens when you throw young players in at the deep end too quickly. Of his victorious 1983 Cup-Winners' Cup side, teenagers John Hewitt, Neil Simpson, Neale Cooper and Eric Black were all later forced to retire prematurely through injury.

"No-one thought any harm was being done at the time," Fergie later explained. "But Manchester United are a bigger club with more resources than Aberdeen, so I'm not under the same sort of pressure to play lads like David Beckham in every game. I can pace them and rest them as they require, not as the team requires."

Also acting as part-time assistant to Scotland manager, Jock Stein, when the Big Man suffered a heart-attack and died during Scotland's qualifying game against Wales for the 1986 World Cup, Fergie agreed to manage the Scottish side through the finals in Mexico.

But it was strictly a temporary arrangement and Fergie would be returning to Aberdeen in time for the new season, he insisted. Both Rangers and Celtic had tried by then to entice him away from Aberdeen, as had English League giants like Arsenal and Leeds. But, he says, Manchester United was "the only club I would ever consider leaving Pittodrie for".

When Ferguson replaced 'Big' Ron Atkinson in 1986, he was dismayed to discover that the best young local talent was more likely to go to Manchester City's nearby School Of Excellence, or even Oldham, than it was to Old Trafford. United had become known as a club that bought its stars ready-made from outside the club.

Fergie's arrival soon changed that. New scouts and coaches were hired, as the boss made it known that from now on only the best was good enough for Manchester United.

His first big scoop was beating Manchester City to the signature of a wiry young lad called Ryan Wilson (son of the Swinton rugby league player, Danny Wilson) who had been terrorising defences in the local junior leagues with his speed and ball-control.

A few months later when his parents separated, the lad changed his surname to his mother's maiden name and became known as Ryan Giggs. When Fergie turned up personally at Ryan's mum's house to try and per-suade her to let her son sign to United, mum duly agreed. It was a decision that neither she, nor her son, nor Alex Ferguson and several million United fans would ever regret.

Becks roars his approval
of another super strike

Beckham quickly
learned to work on
every area of his game –
including his heading

Beckham strides out in an England shirt for the U21s, a valuable learning exercise for top young players

Fergie's first three seasons at Old Trafford may have been a mediocre period for the first team, but as he said on the eve of the FA Cup win, in 1990, which saved his career at Manchester United: "We have a solid base which won't be fully recognised for years to come."

It seemed only fitting that it was one of the earliest, most thrilling products of Fergie's new youth scheme, blonde-haired striker Mark Robbins, who dug a goal out of the mud in the dying minutes of the game to beat Nottingham Forest in the Third Round of the Cup that year. United were struggling near the foot of the League table and had they been knocked out at the first hurdle the rumour mongers suggested that Fergie's job would soon have followed.

Indeed, after United went on to lift the Cup that year, beating Crystal Palace 1-0 in the replay (with a goal by another early Fledgling, left-back Lee Martin), Fergie admitted: "The FA Cup probably saved my job. It would have been easy to sack me. Nobody would have been surprised and I couldn't have complained — I'd had a good crack at it."

By the time David Beckham signed professional forms in 1993, it was the dawn of a new era for Manchester United. The side were on the verge of winning their first League Championship for 26 years, the inspired signing

of Eric Cantona four months into the season providing Fergie with the final piece of a title-winning jigsaw it had taken him nearly seven years to complete.

And while Fergie gloried in being the first man to bring the League Championship to Old Trafford since the days when you could only watch their games on TV in black and white, he took equal satisfaction from the knowledge that the youth-scheme he had implemented seven years before was now coming to such promising fruition.

The A team that thrashed Manchester City 5–1 to win the FA Youth Cup in 1992 contained Beckham, Scholes, Giggs, Butt, Neville, and Keith Gillespie (who later went to Newcastle as part of the £7 million deal that brought Andy Cole to Old Trafford).

As his old rival, Kenny Dalglish, says: "Whatever Fergie's done, he's been successful. He had a bad start at Manchester United and then turned it round completely. Even when the teams weren't doing too well, the foundations were being built."

Becks had made his debut in the United first team earlier in the 1992–3 season, coming on as substitute for Andrei Kanchelskis in a Coca-Cola Cup Second Round tie against Brighton, on September 23 (a draw, thanks to a last-gasp volley from Danny Wallace).

Beckham was rapidly becoming a vital cog in United's engine room — along with Keane and Cantona

Less than two months later, Fergie made the signing that would effectively guarantee success at Old Trafford, bagging Leeds United's French international star, Eric Cantona, for what was, in retrospect, the rock-bottom bargain price of just £1.2 million.

Cantona's influence on the youngsters at Old Trafford went beyond merely inspiring them with his deft touches, cunning flicks and stunning goals.

Away from the cameras and the microphones, Cantona become a mentor to the most promising of the new United youngsters. "Our young players are very good tactically and technically," Cantona declared. "We are playing like a European team... It can progress to win everything."

Becks and the other youth-team players would break-off from training just to watch Eric work-out at The Cliff. Growing up surrounded by stars, still they had never seen anything like the charismatic Frenchman before.

"I could watch him all day," claimed a wide-eyed Becks. "I'd even pay to watch him train. He is unbelievable. All the players look at each other and laugh because they know they couldn't do the things he can do with a ball."

Not that it would stop them from trying ...

Beckham's early international career was handled as carefully as his early days at United

The youngsters
(and David May!)
celebrate...

A GUIDE TO FERGIE'S FLEDGLINGS

NICKY BUTT

His deceptively slight frame belies an array of talents, not least an opportunist's eye for the telling pass, strength in the tackle, and a cool head under pressure that made him an ideal midfield understudy for the battling Paul Ince. Born in Manchester, in 1975, Nicky represented England at Schoolboy, Under-18, and Under-21 levels, and was in the side with Becks in the FA Youth Cup victory of 1992. He made his first team debut for United against Oldham when he was 18.

GARY NEVILLE

Born in Bury, in 1975, Gary joined United as a trainee the same time as Becks. A multi-talented defender who can play anywhere, but who Fergie sees long-term as a centre-back, Gary made his League debut against Coventry City in May 1994. A 'veteran', at 21, of the England Euro 96 side, he is another "old head on young shoulders," as Hoddle would say.

PHILIP NEVILLE

Younger by a year than his brother — he didn't sign professional forms for United until July 1994. But as Gary says, "Philip was noticed more when he was younger." Another versatile defender, he had played for England Schoolboys and the Manchester United Youth teams when he was 15. And he later captained the A team that beat Tottenham in the 1995 FA Youth Cup final. Philip made his first-team debut in the 1995 FA Cup against Wrexham and is now a full England international, where he has been converted into a wing-half.

PAUL SCHOLES

The only one of the new wave of United stars that really comes close to rivalling the extravagant skills of the boy Beckham though. Born in Salford, Goalsey Scholesy was already an England Youth International when he signed professional forms for United at the same time as Becks. Another member of the FA Youth Cup-winning side of 1992 (he scored a hat-trick), Paul was always a prolific goal scorer. When he made his Premiership debut, against Ipswich, at Portman Road, in 1994, coming on as a substitute for Lee Sharpe, he scored 12 minutes later! And he scored on his full England debut, in the 2–0 victory over Italy in last summer's Le Tournoi de France

PHIL MULRYNE

19-year-old, Belfast-born winger who has already made his debut for Northern Ireland (against Belgium at Windsor Park, the Irish winning 3–0. Mulryne scored one and made another with an inch-perfect cross after a terrific run down the wing) though he has yet to make the first team squad at United! A friend of former United Youth team star, Keith Gillespie (who set up his goal), and similar in style.

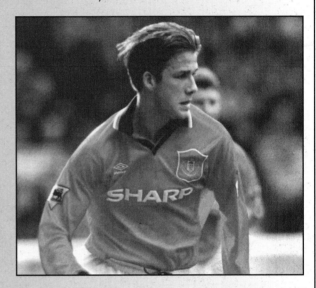

On the lookout for his young team-mates

BEN THORNLEY

A brilliant new striker who appeared on the bench for several of United's first-team games in the 1996–7 season and will surely be knocking on the door next term.

JOHN CURTIS

An outstanding young defender (said to be 'the new Duncan Edwards'), who captains the Youth A team. He also played for England's Under-18 side for the first time at the end of the 1996–7 season — a friendly against Scotland at Gigg Lane which finished 4–1 to England, with John bagging the fourth with a header!

WES BROWN AND JAMIE WOOD

Also represented in the England Under-18 side. Both supremely talented ball-players that can play in midfield or upfront. Tellingly, no other club provide more than one player for the England side.

Double Vision

The name David Beckham first began to appear regularly on the Manchester United first team-sheet in the 1994–5 season. Having just won their second Premiership title in a row and completed a remarkable Double by also winning the FA Cup (beating Chelsea 4–0 in a thrilling final at Wembley), this was never going to be an easy team for the 19-year-old Becks to break into.

Featuring stars like Cantona, Kanchelskis, Sharpe, Hughes, Ince, Giggs and Keane, Becks knew patience would be his biggest virtue over the coming months. After retaining the Charity Shield, beating Blackburn 2–0 courtesy of a typically cool penalty from Cantona and a superb overhead kick from Ince, United's Premier League season began in earnest with another 2–0 victory, at home to QPR.

Alex Ferguson was determined to see United mount a serious challenge on the European Champions Cup, but with the three-foreigners-only rule still in place, combined with a daunting domestic fixture list, Fergie decided to experiment when it came to the early rounds of both the European Champions League and the Coca-Cola Cup.

Which is how, six months before he would make his Premiership debut, Becks was included on the team-sheet, as a sub in United's opening match of their European campaign, at home to IFK Gothenburg.

Beckham came into the
United side on the crest of
their success – and took them
on to new heights

Becks takes a breather during a cold day's training

Giggs (twice), Kanchelskis and Sharpe got the goals in a blinding 4-2 victory, and though he didn't come on, Becks learned something that night about the atmosphere of Old Trafford on the big European occasions, and what would be expected of him if and when he was called from the bench.

Seven days later, Becks was in the starting line-up for the first time at Number 7 for the away leg of United's Second Round Coca-Cola Cup tie against Port Vale, along with most of the team that had won the FA Youth Cup two years before – none of them yet 20.

Port Vale complained about United fielding an "under-strength side" and put in a formal complaint

has vision and an incredible passing ability that United often lack, even in their awesome first-team line-up."

The following week, Becks was back on the subs bench for United's away visit to fearsome Turkish champions, Galatasaray. He didn't play in the tense 0-0 draw, but the experience was invaluable. There are few atmospheres more intimidating than the emotional cauldron of the Ali Sami Yen Stadium, and Becks began to wonder what it would be like to play against a team like the Turks. He would find out sooner than he thought.

Becks was again one of six players still in their teens for the return-leg against Port Vale. The FA threatened to levy

" Beckham has incredible passing ability..."

to the FA, but Paul Scholes got both the goals in a nifty 2-1 win.

"Choccy is their teacher!" the United fans sang, referring to Brian McClair – with Keane and Irwin, the only first-team members present that night. And the papers were full of it the next day. "They were the kids off the Old Trafford block that had produced nothing like it since Matt Busby's glorious era of English domination," trumpeted *The Sun*. While *Today* singled Becks out for special praise: "David Beckham

a £50,000 fine on the club for fielding a 'weakened' side but United won easily, 2-0, while the crowd sang: "They go to school in the morning!"

Becks was in the starting line-up again for the away-tie at Newcastle in the next round, on October 26, as Fergie kept his word and played 'the kids' that had beaten Port Vale, with only Irwin, Bruce, Pallister and McClair from the first team in the side. For 80 enthralling, action-packed minutes, they held their own against a full-strength

Newcastle side desperate to avoid the humiliation of losing to Fergie's Fledglings. Then, with two well-taken goals in five minutes from Philippe Albert and Paul Kitson, Newcastle were through.

There was no cause for disappointment at Old Trafford. *The Daily Express* said it best: "Newcastle's vastly more experienced line-up had more than their fair share of the early play, but it was the sweet, uninhibited football of Fergie's Fledglings that made the senses tingle."

Becks was on the subs bench again for the away trip to Barcelona on November 2, wearing the Number 13 shirt — unlucky for some. Certainly United's luck seemed to have run out that night, as Barcelona ran riot in a spectacular 4–0 victory. But watching players close-up of the calibre of Hristo Stoichkov and Romario, both of whom scored that night, was a lesson in itself.

Becks was back on the bench for United's next European tie — a forlorn 3–1 defeat away to IFK Gothenburg, which effectively ended their European campaign — before finally getting his break in the final home-tie against Galatasaray, on December 7. Becks seized his opportunity, playing out of his skin and outshining even his mentor, Cantona, on the night.

Simon Davies had opened the scoring after just two minutes. Then, in the 38th minute, Cantona stroked an inch-perfect pass into Beckham's path, who ran at the goal before unleashing a dipping shot from 20 yards which flew into the net. Keane cracked in a third at the start of the second half and an unlucky own-goal by centre-half Karkmaz Bulent made it 4–0.

United were out of Europe but it felt like the start of something big for Beckham. Would the new boy-star Fergie had unveiled against Galatasaray now become a feature of the first-team for Premiership matches?

Not yet, said Fergie. "Young talent must be introduced carefully, in stages, not sucked dry prematurely by over-exposure."

But with the manager keen that his young star keep his match-fitness, Becks was given a loan spell at Preston, in January 1995, where he played in four games and scored once — a typically spectacular goal straight from a corner!

Becks found himself hurriedly recalled to Old Trafford at the end of the month, however, when the biggest story of the season broke: Eric Cantona's 'kung-fu' attack on a member of the crowd at Selhurst Park after being sent-off during a 1–1 draw with Crystal Palace. His punishment: a nine-month, worldwide ban from playing that many predicted would end his career in English football.

As we now know, Cantona would return to Old Trafford the following season, having served over 100 hours of Community Service (coaching football to underprivileged kids), and ready to lead the team to an historic second Double. But all of that was far from

Taking a pot-shot from outside the box

certain as United fought on without their best player through the last weeks of the 1994–5 season.

Becks' Premiership debut finally came at Old Trafford on April 2, against Leeds. Wearing the Number 14 shirt usually sported by the injured Kanchelskis, he turned in a solid, unfussy performance in a bitter 0–0 draw.

At the end, Leeds fans chanted: "You're not the champions anymore". It would go to the last game before it was true, but the writing was on the wall as Blackburn surged ahead. Becks was to make four further appearances in the Premiership that season — as a sub against Leicester, Coventry and Southampton, and once from the start against Chelsea (though he was subbed at half-time) — but like United, Becks's season began to fizzle out.

He started the match in both quarter and semi-finals of the 1995 FA Cup run, but Becks admits he struggled. Butt replaced him for the second-half of the semi-final against Crystal Palace, at Villa Park. United fought hard for their 2–2 draw, coming back twice in extra-time with goals from Irwin and Pallister. But Becks didn't make the squad for the replay three days later, a 2–0 win for United, again at Villa Park.

And that, sadly, was it. A heart-rending 1–1 draw at West Ham on the final day of the season handed the Premiership title to Blackburn, and the disappointing 1–0 defeat to Everton at Wembley put paid to their FA Cup hopes.

It was a bitter end to a season that had started so brightly for both Beckham and United. But Becks rightfully preferred to dwell on the positive. He had broken into the first-team and now, just turned 20, he intended to stay there. Apart from his own undeniable talent, the chief reason Becks got his chance at a more permanent position in the team at the start of the 1995–6 season was the manager's shock decision — widely debated in the press — to sell three of his biggest stars.

Definitely an Under-21: Baby-faced Beckham steps out for his country for one of the first times...

The sudden loss of Mark Hughes to Chelsea, Paul Ince to Inter Milan, and Andrei Kanchelskis to Everton left many United fans distraught at what they saw as the manager's premature breaking-up of the original Double-winning side. Stranger still, Fergie made no move to buy replacements. The only signing that summer was the £500,000 purchase of Manchester City goalie Tony Coton, as cover for Schmeichel.

When United lost 3–1 away at Aston Villa on the opening day of the new season, they felt their worst fears were being realised. Becks came on for Philip Neville at half-time, with United trailing 3–0, and scored his first goal for the senior side — a scorching 25-yard volley that left Villa keeper Mark Bosnich standing. But that didn't stop the critics predicting doom and gloom for United in the forthcoming season unless Fergie got his cheque-book out quick.

Alan Hansen made his famous, "You can't win anything with kids," comment that night on *Match Of The Day*, and the only person who disagreed with him was Alex Ferguson, who pointed out that his senior players had also played fitfully that day. Hansen, said Fergie, "gets a bit excited about Manchester United, maybe because of the old Liverpool thing. It affects him a wee bit."

Sure enough, after that shock beginning, the new young United team settled into its stride. At one point before Cantona made his comeback, Scholesy had scored eight goals in seven games, and though they were not top of the table, they trailed leaders Newcastle by just a handful of points.

There was no excuse, however, for their embarrassing capitulation 3–0 at home to lowly York City, in the Second Round first-leg of the Coca-Cola Cup. They avenged themselves by winning the return 3–1 but it was not enough to stop United tumbling out of the competition, red-faced, at the first hurdle.

Most disconcerting of all was their equally unexpected expulsion from the UEFA Cup at the hands of First Round opponents Rotor Volograd. Having obtained a credible 0–0 draw in Russia, they were two goals down by half-time at home in the second-leg, and only equalised late in the game — first from Scholes, on the hour, and then, a minute from time, from a Schmeichel header! — but went out on the away goals rule.

Cantona's return to the first team for their home game against Liverpool on October 1 was a watershed: a hard-fought 2–2 draw which heralded the beginning of a double comeback for both the club and Cantona. With Old Trafford awash with French *tricolore* flags, Cantona launched a beautifully executed cross that found Butt on the edge of the Liverpool penalty area. He swivelled past a startled Phil Babb before volleying home to give United an early lead.

And it was another perfectly angled Cantona pass, after Liverpool had fought back to lead 2–1, that put Giggs

Head down, eye on the ball: Beckham's great technique gives him power and accuracy

Stretching out in England colours

through for a straight run at goal. Brought down inside the box in desperation by Jamie Redknapp, Cantona calmly stroked home the resulting penalty to a tumultuous roar from the Old Trafford faithful.

Cantona was the talisman around which United hung their hopes. Becks, Scholes, Butt and the Nevilles were coming on in leaps and bounds, but to have Cantona there amongst them, not just on the field, but talking quietly and taking time to explain things in the dressing room afterwards, was an invaluable asset.

Fergie remembers coming into the dressing room an hour after the game against Galatasaray had finished and finding Eric with Becks and Gary Neville at the tactics board together, the younger players all ears as the enigmatic Frenchman discussed his ideas.

"Eric, Peter Schmeichel, Roy Keane and Gary Pallister all helped us through," confirms Gary Neville. "Now, I think, we are in a position to help them."

Not everybody was thrilled to see the return of the 'disgraced' star, though. Before the match against Bolton in February, police announced that a £10,000 'reward' had been put up by some local thugs for anyone who could "get" Cantona. Security was considerably tightened at Burnden Park that day, but the only ones who 'got' Cantona were the Bolton defence, whom he swirled past to provide passes for Becks (after five minutes), Butt, Bruce, Scholes (twice) and Cole to notch up a crushing 6–0 victory!

Kevin Keegan's Newcastle were the team to beat this year, the side ironically comprising both a former Manchester United Youth team star of their own, in Keith Gillespie, and a flamboyant French international too, in David Ginola.

Together, they tore defences apart for Les Ferdinand to put the ball in the net. By the start of the new year, Newcastle had a 12-point lead over United. Then Keegan

decided to splash out on two players, Blackburn's David Batty and Parma's Colombian star Faustino Asprilla. These purchases plus injuries to key players may have been factors that enabled United to move back above Newcastle in the table by mid-April.

But it was the 13 wins in 17 games on the run-in that really did the job for United — Cantona scoring six goals in six games as United took 16 points from their last 18 to overhaul Newcastle in the last stages of the race.

Through it all, as United closed the gap, Becks' performances grew stronger, his 32 League matches and seven Cup ties that season peppered with eight goals, nearly all scored from outside the box. The media were quick to pick up on the new boy-wonder, comparing him to everybody from Glenn Hoddle to Paul Gascoigne.

Some knowledgeable critics went so far as comparing Becks to the great Duncan Edwards. Frank Taylor, the only surviving journalist of nine UK correspondents that were on the fateful flight from Munich, recalled that the Germans rechristened Duncan 'Boom Boom' Edwards because, "he was likely to score from 30 or 40 yards out. Beckham is the nearest thing in the modern game."

The killer punch for United was their decisive 1–0 defeat of Newcastle at St James Park, in March — another last-minute Cantona goal that left United just one point behind the Magpies. Becks had been a substitute for that one, but he was back again for the crucial home tie against Leeds. A fiercely-contested battle was settled by a Keane goal. After the match, Fergie's angry comments about the enormous effort from Leeds compared to some of their other performances provoked a bitter response from Keegan.

"I'll tell you something, he went down in my estimation when he said that," Keegan spluttered on Sky. "And I'll tell you honestly, I will love it if we beat them — love it!"

Europe became another
arena in which Beckham
had to learn fast

Del Piero and Dechamps of Juventus bear down on Beckham as the three internationals fight it out

If Fergie, the master of psychology, had intended to unsettle his opponent, he had hit the bullseye. But by then, United were back in the driving seat anyway. The two scintillating goals Becks scored in the 5—0 thrashing of Nottingham Forest for United's last home game of the season left them in an almost unassailable position at the top of the table. And the 3—0 victory at Middlesbrough's new Riverside stadium a few days later was enough to confirm what everybody already knew: that Premiership trophy would be going back to Old Trafford for the third time in four years.

Beckham's own most memorable goal of the season was his brilliant last-minute winner against Chelsea in the semi-final of the FA Cup. A Cole header had cancelled-out an early Chelsea strike, then, two minutes from time, Becks picked up a loose ball on the edge of the area, coolly slotted it into the net, and United were in the FA Cup final for the third year running.

Their opponents this year, Liverpool, were widely tipped to take revenge on their rivals by denying them an historic second Double and for most of the match United were forced to defend.

Becks was impressive throughout, totally unfazed by the enormity of the occasion. He even came close to scoring when he blazed a 20-yard missile at the goal which David James dived heroically to push aside.

Then, with five minutes remaining on the clock and the match looking certain to go to extra-time, United got a corner on the right. Becks swung it over and James leapt to meet it but could only manage to punch the ball as far as Cantona, poised on the edge of the box. Taking half a pace backwards, he balanced himself perfectly and struck the ball first time, a volley that rifled its way through the packed penalty area and into the back of the Liverpool net.

"You'll never win the Double with kids!" sang the delighted United hordes, emphasising the scale of Fergie's and United's astonishing achievement. The only club in history to do the Double — twice! It was, said England coach Terry Venables, "so stunning it's almost unbelievable".

'Formi-double!' went one headline the next day, catching the mood exactly. Nothing could spoil the moment when Cantona lifted the trophy from the Duchess of Kent — not even when the lid fell off and went rolling down the steps.

Becks and the rest of the kids of United had written their way into United's most astonishing success story for 30 years. But it was the oldest kid on the block himself, Alex Ferguson, that got and deserved the last word.

"The real achievement was how well and how long the young players lasted," he said in summing up an incredible year. "Our Double triumph is as much a victory for youth as it is for Manchester United."

More Juve action: United must now prove themselves against the best in Europe

Power, pace and
poise: all part of
the Beckham game

A thoughtful moment before
the battle commences

Spends and Spice Girls

You don't have to be a Manchester United supporter to be a David Beckham fan. The headline-grabbing goals he scores and the youthful, fun-loving persona that he projects has made Becks the idol of teenage boys and the pin-up of teenage girls everywhere. Such is his popularity these days that Becks is now the top-selling name in the Manchester United merchandising shop, replacing Cantona, who is still second, followed by Schmeichel and Giggs.

Friends say success hasn't changed Beckham one bit, it's just the way other people look at him now that is different. So what is Becks the bloke like away from the crowd? What is it that makes him tick once the match is over?

"We still have the same friends, eat the same food and go to bed at the same time," says Philip Neville. "We've just got better cars and houses, but that's the reward for sacrificing so much when we were younger. People say that footballers have an easy life, and it's true to some extent, but from the age of 14 to 18 you give your life to football and miss out on the things other teenagers do."

Ryan Giggs, who was also forced to grow up in the spotlight, agrees: "It can be tough watching mates who are not in the game really enjoying themselves when you have to stay disciplined. I definitely envy them that freedom at times."

Becks is no different. He likes a few beers with the lads

David and girlfriend Victoria 'Posh Spice' Adams don't get much time together, so they make the most of it when they do...

Beckham's good looks have raised his profile even higher — and attracted the attention of Posh Spice...

occasionally, or a glass of wine with a meal. But never more than once a week. "You have to take care of yourself at this level," he says.

Besides, going out since he became famous is not always easy. When he and some of the other United lads went to see Oasis play at Maine Road, "it wasn't that enjoyable," Becks admits. They had come straight from beating Forest 5–0 and "we had to watch our backs all night," because of constant harassment from envious Manchester City fans.

"The adulation is just part of the job," Becks says philosophically. "If you are going to be in the public eye, you are bound to get stared at and the signing of autographs and talking to people is no problem. I can remember going to West Ham when United were playing there and getting autographs of Bryan Robson and Gordon Strachan. I even got Glenn Hoddle to sign my Under-21 shirt."

Dealing with the media, though, was something else. "When you're young it can be a daunting prospect," he admits. "They can be very clever with their words. I have been on a media course to try and help me deal with it."

Even so, sometimes, "it's got right out of hand. It's hard enough dealing with the attention you get on the sports pages, but when people start plastering you over pages three and four because you've turned up at some function or other, that's when it gets ridiculous."

Fortunately, Becks likes to keep both feet on the ground. "There's no way I can get carried away, especially with our boss Alex Ferguson. He didn't let it happen with Ryan Giggs and now he's doing his stuff with the rest of the young players coming through."

Off the pitch United players are expected to be ambassadors for the club and Fergie still makes Becks and the others get their hair cut when he thinks its getting too long.

And the manager discourages his younger players from spending too much time on outside interests. While the young stars of Liverpool were being photographed living it up in nightclubs in the 1995–6 season, Becks, Scholes, Butt and the Nevilles were seldom seen outside the club. Some dubbed Old Trafford 'Colditz', but United did another Double.

Jetting in: David and Victoria return from a trip abroad

Suited up and testing
the Wembley turf
with Andy Cole
before the 1996
FA Cup final

Cream of the crop: The players of the year, Beckham, Shearer and Beardsley, collect their trophies

However, with Becks now over 21, he is free to make his own choices. At the start of 1997, he signed a five-year contract with United reputedly worth in the region of £1.5 million, plus an exclusive, six-year sponsorship deal with Adidas.

"It's a bit of pocket money and it buys a few clothes," he says bashfully. "At least I don't have to buy my own boots any more."

Not that he's about to throw away the "lucky boots" he always wears for training. He's far too superstitious. "I always wear the same pair for training, but for every international match I wear a new pair and for United I change them every two or three games. The rest of the kit is supplied."

On the old Stretford End, there was a popular theory, stretching back to the days of George Best and his right-wing twin, Willie Morgan, that United never took on a player that wasn't good-looking. And Becks is doing his best to keep up that tradition, spending nearly as much time in front of the mirror gelling his hair as discussing tactics. He sometimes wears designer-specs off the pitch as well, but insists they are not just another fashion accessory (he wears them for driving and watching TV).

Like most 22-year-olds, Becks buys a lot of CDs — anything from Bryan Adams to Oasis, though his favourite is usually Simply Red's 'Greatest Hits'. But he says his main interests outside football revolve around "clothes and cars". Becks owns a BMW and an electric-blue Mercedes,

and he recently bought himself a large house. "I need one to keep all my clothes in," he jokes. "I think I spend most of my money on clothes, although recently I've had a thing about watches."

Latterly, he's even begun modelling in magazines and on the catwalk. "I get quite a bit of stick from the United lads for it! It's like a hobby to me, really ... If I'm not at the club, you will probably find me in the city looking for some new stuff for my wardrobe."

It's a look that has not gone unnoticed. "It's only in the last two years I've realised they're such a sexy team," frothed TV presenter Zoe Ball, who dropped her life-long allegiance to Liverpool to become a Manchester United fan. "David Beckham — oohhh!" she squealed. She even bought a satellite dish just so she could watch United on Sky Sports.

By the start of 1997, Becks was beginning to be seen as something of an item on the celebrity pages himself when he was photographed taking the stunning Italian Vogue model, Stephanie Lyra, out on several dates — with onlookers remarking on how 'affectionate' they were in public.

That didn't stop other girls falling at his feet, though. Quite literally, in the case of his current girlfriend, Victoria 'Posh Spice' Adams of the Spice Girls, who says she was first attracted to Becks because of the £250 Gucci loafers he was wearing (she's always had a thing about men in loafers, especially her favourite designer brand, Gucci). Not that Becks was wearing any socks at the time. In fact, Vicky was

A European work-out by night. You can still feel the magic...

Things have happened fast
for David since he broke into
the United side — but he's
remained level-headed

Training remains a point of focus for David: Fergie makes sure the players continue to work for their success

lucky she found him in shoes at all, his usual habit being to either go barefoot or with just a flimsy pair of beach-sandals on.

The Sun broke the story, under the front-page heading: Posh Spice Nets Man U David. "She's a nice girl," Becks was quoted as saying. "And we had a nice time." But a pal told the paper: "They hit it off as soon as they met — they really enjoy each other's company." The same age, they first met after United's home game against Sheffield Wednesday, which the Spice Girls were guests at, in March. After the match, which United won 2–0, Becks and Giggsy thought they'd have a laugh and take 'Posh' (Victoria) and 'Scary' (Melanie Brown) Spice out for dinner, and then on to a club.

Since then, Becks and Vicky have been seen dancing together into the early hours, ensconced together in the exclusive VIP section of London's trendy Emporium nightclub. Or spotted driving to her parents' luxury home, in Kent, in her purple MG convertible.

A friend said: "David knows about Victoria's ex-boyfriend and has helped her through a tough time. He's always there if she wants to talk and he's an excellent listener. He also appreciates the pressures that sudden stardom can bring."

When Victoria went to America with the Spice Girls not long after they met, Becks was never off his mobile to her — even when United arrived in Germany for their European Cup semi-final against Borussia Dortmund. Meanwhile, in New York, Victoria was being teased by the other Spice Girlies for behaving "like a besotted teenager" over the United star.

Because of their commitments, they see each other rarely, so they always make the most of what little time they have together. Before England's World Cup qualifying game against Poland, in May, Vicky whisked Becks off for dinner one night — in Italy. "He's so special, I just had to take him away for dinner," she told reporters.

Becks extended his current "thing" for watches when he paid a reported £10,000 for a white gold timepiece for Victoria.

Now there is even talk of the couple getting married. When asked right out by fans as they signed autographs together outside her parents' house recently, Becks refused to confirm or deny the rumours. He just stood there in his sandals and dark-glasses, grinning. "I have taken so much stick over that from the lads," Becks said later. "They all want to be my best man."

It's a relationship that has helped propel Beckham from the back-pages to the front far quicker than any of his goals could, and with it have come new pressures.

"I feel sorry for Becks because at the moment everybody wants to find something on him," says Gary Neville, his best friend at United. "He's just going to have to live with that because he's become so successful."

Becks rooms with Gary when they're on England trips, but has his own room for away games with United, as Gary

Playing for Manchester
United and buying
clothes: the things that
keep Becks happy!

shares with his brother. Becks used to room with Lee Sharpe, whom he has now, ironically, replaced in the United starting line-up. "He was always great fun to be around. I think he was quite unique in his way... I miss Steve Bruce as well, but more for his encouragement and strength in the changing room."

Being called up for the England squad has changed his outlook on things. On England trips, the League doesn't get mentioned much amongst the other players. "I think that's just out of courtesy," says Becks. But the team spirit is always high. "People like Gazza, Incey and Ian Wright make sure of that."

Liverpool's Jamie Redknapp has become another big mate of Becks' on England trips — both young, both the pin-ups of their respective sides, both fluid midfielders no stranger to the telling cross-field pass or shot at goal from 30 yards out. And, most important of all, as Becks says, "We get on well together."

Other England pals are fellow youngsters in the squad like Tottenham defender Sol Campbell, Everton defender David Unsworth, and Everton forward Nicky Barmby. They tend to play golf together, or snooker. Or just watch telly. Usually for the sports coverage (as long as it's not cricket — which Becks "hates"), or some comedy — Becks' favourites are the *Harry Enfield Show* and *Only Fools And Horses*.

Outside the game, one of his closest new mates is snooker ace and fellow Londoner, Ronnie O'Sullivan. "I met him in London a few years ago," says Becks. "We're both from London and we've got the same sort of humour." Boxing champion, Prince Naseem, whom Becks took part in a photo-shoot with at the St Thomas's gym in Sheffield where Naz trains, is another "mate".

Becks says he hasn't really thought a great deal yet about how he would like the rest of his life and career to go. "As long as I'm happy and I can still buy clothes, that'll do me."

And if the seers of Serie A should come a-calling? He is honest enough to admit that, "I wouldn't mind going abroad, but it's just that I am so happy with United and want to stay here ... I don't think there's that much difference between the Premiership and Serie A and I want to win more things with United."

England's Dreaming

With England's thrilling run to the semi-finals of the 1996 European Championships, football had gripped the country's imagination in a way that had not been seen since the national team won the World Cup 30 years before. And with stars like Ravanelli, Vialli, Zola, Juninho, Bergkamp, Asprilla, Vieira and Cantona all poised to make this the most exciting Premiership season yet, 1996–7 promised much for United's young double-Double winners, and demanded more.

Behind the scenes, fond farewells were bid to yet more members of the original 1994 Double-winning side: Lee Sharpe (transferred to Leeds Utd), Paul Parker (to Derby County) and captain Steve Bruce (to Birmingham City). And for the first time in two years, Fergie went out and bought several new faces — Norwegian defender, Ronny Johnsen, and striker Ole Gunnar Solskjaer; Czech Republic midfield tyro Karel Poborsky; plus Dutch forward Jordi Cruyff, and goalie, Raimond Van der Gouw — all of whom had caught Fergie's eagle-eye during Euro 96.

For Becks and the other four members of what the press were now calling 'the Famous Five' (the Nevilles, Butt and Scholes), the coming season would also provide them with their biggest test yet.

As Philip Neville acknowledged: "The second season is always the hardest. Other players get to know your weaknesses and strengths, so we'll have to work even harder."

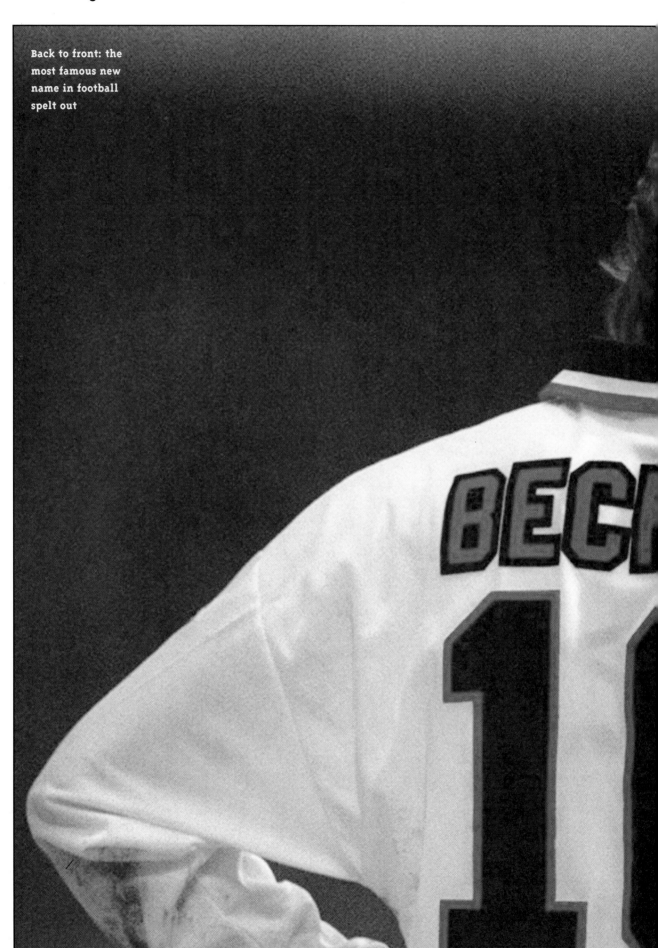

Back to front: the
most famous new
name in football
spelt out

Becks has power as well as skill in his array of talents

It was doubly reassuring then to see Becks start the season as he meant to go on — scoring in United's opening day 4–0 thrashing of Newcastle in the Charity Shield. But of course it was his unbelievable 57-yard strike against Wimbledon on the opening day of the season that really set the tone for Becks' most sensational year yet.

"My season changed completely after that goal," he recalls. "It was definitely the watershed for me. After that, I seemed to be scoring in every match in the first half of the season. I kept saying to myself, surely I can't get another goal. But I did. I now feel I can handle anything. I am comfortable wherever I play."

The cherry on the cake came a few days later when Becks was named in Glenn Hoddle's first ever England squad. Hoddle cheerfully admitted the Wimbledon goal had influenced his choice. It was, he said, "a wonderful piece of skill that elevated him a bit quicker than he might otherwise have been. He is a talented player and it took him a couple of rungs up the ladder quickly. That happens when you score special goals. People will remember them, not the simple tap-ins."

Indeed, Hoddle was so impressed he decided to give a full debut to Beckham in England's crucial opening World Cup qualifying fixture away to Moldova, on September 1. England won 3–0 and Becks, playing wide on the right, repaid the new manager's faith in him with a fine cross for

Nicky Barmby to score the decisive goal. After the match, Beckham was buzzing.

"Getting called up by Glenn Hoddle — a man I've always admired — was one thing," says Becks. "But then making my debut was something else. It was absolutely incredible! I don't think I'll ever experience anything like it again."

In fact, it was just six weeks before Becks would get the chance to do just that when he was again selected for the starting line-up for England's next World Cup qualifying game, away to Georgia, on November 11. England won 2–0 and Becks gave another convincing performance. He was again played wide on the right as opposed to in his usual role for United in the central midfield. But already he was being compared to a young Bobby Charlton, another central midfield general who began on the wing for England.

Back home, United's season was gathering momentum. They had been bumped out of the Coca-Cola Cup by former United captain Bryan Robson's Middlesbrough, and would be unexpectedly nudged from their throne in the FA Cup by gritty Wimbledon, but domestically, they continued to rule the roost.

Liverpool were breathing down their necks, but a Becks screamer from 20 yards at Old Trafford in October gave United three points and an important psychological advantage that the Merseysiders were never able to fully overcome.

United's white knight:
heading for another
title at full tilt

Beckham faced up to the demands of a hard club season, Euro campaign and England games with style

United's march towards their fourth Premiership title in five years was peppered with brilliant performances and important goals from their new No 10. The game away to Spurs, in January, was a typical example. With 12 minutes to go and the match heading for a 1—1 stalemate, Becks picked up the ball in his own half and, from 30 yards out, unleashed a cannon of a shot which left Ian Walker gaping and United three crucial points the better off.

He had done almost the same thing in United's 2—0 FA Cup Third Round victory over Spurs a week before. "I know what Beckham can do but stopping him is a different story," said the Tottenham and England goalie. "You know the shot is coming but you can't stop it. Anyone can get lucky and hit the top corner, but it's more than that with him. He does it so regularly, you know if you give him space and time he can destroy you."

More proof of the ability of Fergie's new, young side came when they beat Arsenal 2—1 at Highbury in February, without Cantona to help them. The pace and passing of Becks and the goals of Cole and Solskjaer destroyed the Gunners' fading title hopes.

But the decisive blow was delivered at Anfield itself, on April 20, when two powerfully in-swinging corners from

Becks gave Gary Pallister the chance to head United 2—1 up. Cole finished the Scousers off in the second half with a header for 3—1, and afterwards Liverpool manager Roy Evans, admitted "It was a massive blow for us."

It was also both Beckham's and United's best season, so far, in the European Champions League, despite getting off to a fitful start — a 1—0 defeat away to Juventus which could have seen the Italian holders score five, followed by an encouraging 2—0 victory at home to Rapid Vienna.

Things had picked up with a surprise 2—0 victory away to Fenerbahce. But two further home defeats, both 1—0, to Fenerbahce (the first time United had ever been beaten at home in Europe), and then Juventus (a Butt tackle on Del Piero resulting in a penalty) meant United needed to win their final Group C match away to Rapid Vienna on December 4 to qualify for the quarter-finals. Even then, an unlikely away victory for Fenerbahce the same night against Juventus would put United out whatever the result.

It was a tremendous match, United pressing from the start before Rapid suddenly broke back with a shot that forced a magnificently athletic save from Schmeichel that stood comparison to the legendary save Gordon Banks made against Pele of Brazil in the 1970 World Cup.

Full International:
And so proud to
wear the shirt

Beckham relaxed quickly into the swing of things under Hoddle — and liked his approach to the game

Then, after 23 minutes, Cantona sent the ball skidding into the path of Giggs whose shot catapulted it into the net. 15 minutes from the end, Becks made sure, sending over a beautifully weighted cross after another mazy run to leave Cantona a simple header into the net. 2—0, and with Juventus winning by the same score, United were through to the quarter-finals for the first time since 1969.

"We deserved to win here," said an exultant Fergie afterwards. "And our players will be better for the experience."

Prophetic words, for as we now know, both Becks and United produced their most commanding performance of the season when they met their quarter-final opponents, Porto, in the first leg at Old Trafford, on March 5.

Despite the threats from Jardel, the Brazilian striker whose goals had demolished AC Milan and who claimed he would "turn Old Trafford to ice", United slaughtered the Portuguese champions 4—0. At the heart of a superb United performance were Beckham and Giggs.

On the charge: United eventually retained their title comfortably. It may not be as easy next time...

The Guardian called it, "an absolutely bloody marvellous, incredibly achieved miracle." Fergie called it a result that was "beyond my dreams and probably everyone else's too... I would have been happy with 1–0 but 4–0 is fantastic." With the return-leg — a nervy 0–0 draw — practically a formality, Becks looked forward eagerly to United's semi-final against the German Champions, Borussia Dortmund.

Sadly, Dortmund would prove too strong for United, beating them fairly and squarely 1–0 both home and away. At the time, it was seen as a great disappointment, United missing so many chances — including a goal-line clearance from a Becks shot — they blamed themselves for the defeat rather than the skill of the opposition.

But when you consider that Dortmund would go on to pulverise holders and hot-favourites Juventus 3–1 in the final a month later, United can hold their heads high. They came this close to beating the eventual European Champions, and as Fergie said, putting a brave face on it for ITV after the match: "There's always next year."

And so there would be. United were confirmed as Premiership Champions with just 71 points and two games to go, when Liverpool lost 2–1 at Wimbledon and Newcastle could only draw 0–0 at relegation-threatened West Ham. But as Fergie pointed out: "It was the two victories against Arsenal and the two against Liverpool that have really won it for us."

United's final game of the season, a 2–0 victory at home to West Ham, was a celebratory occasion. Becks managed to shut his ears from the Posh Spice taunts from the Hammers hardcore long enough to set up the first goal in the 12th minute — another powerful in-swinging corner, half-cleared as far as Scholesy who launched a power-drive that struck the bar and hit the line — Solskjaer, the 'Baby Faced Assassin', heading in.

For good measure, United's Reserves also won the Pontin's League and their A and B Youth teams both won their respective Lancashire Leagues, too. Champions all, from tip to toe, all the teams celebrated in time-honoured style with bottles of bubbly and much horse-play for a photo-session at The Cliff the next day, wearing sky-blue track suits as if to placate the rest of Manchester's footballing public.

Powering United
to more glory:
Beckham is now a
major star

Becks ended the season third top scorer,with nine, behind Cantona's 11 and Solskjaer's 17. More importantly perhaps, he proved that he could take the pressure. As *The Independent* noted: "12 months ago he was not sure of his place in the first-team. Now he is their creative lynchpin."

"This last year has been unbelievable for me but even so, I never thought I would get this much attention," said Becks. "I've always known I was capable of scoring goals, but I never thought I was going to score quite as many as I have this season.

"The more you score, the more people expect you to score. The fact that I've not exactly scored tap-ins doesn't help matters either. It's actually got to the stage now where people on the sidelines are screaming, 'Shoot! Shoot!' — and that's when I'm in my own half!"

In recognition of an exceptional season, on April 13, Becks was voted Young Player of the Year by the Professional Footballers Association — the highest accolade possible from his fellow players. Incredibly, Becks also came second in the actual Player Of The Year category, only beaten by Alan Shearer, whose goals at Euro 96 understandably tipped the balance in his favour. (Becks had already won Sky TV's Young Player of the Year award in January.)

Receiving the award at the PFA's plush annual dinner at London's Grosvenor House, Becks said: "When you look at some of the players nominated, the likes of Robbie Fowler and Emile Heskey, you think to yourself, 'Do people really think I'm that good?'"

Peter Beardsley, who also picked up a special merit award from the PFA honouring his 'outstanding contribution to football', said: "David's got everything, a big heart, big engine and scores great goals. I [first] played against him two-and-a-half years ago, and it was obvious he would be special." Becks would handle the recognition and the fame, predicted the Newcastle and former England star. "He had his dad here tonight."

Nevertheless, Becks admits that, "sometimes it's difficult to take in. One day I'm working hard to establish myself in the game and the next I'm playing in front of 55,000 fans at Old Trafford. To then get called up by England is, well, it's hard to put into words really."

These days Beckham, Scholes, Butt and both Nevilles are all regular names in the full England squad — indeed, Gary Neville won his 20th England cap when he played in the acclaimed 2—0 victory away to Poland in the World Cup qualifier, in May.

But Becks continues to be the focus of all England's future hopes. Hoddle says he thinks Beckham could become "the jewel in the crown" of the England side that will play at the 1998 World Cup in France. "He has got a very mature head and he is an accomplished player at a very young age with a lot of experience under his belt."

His was one of the few bright performances in England's grey 1—0 defeat to Italy, at Wembley last February, when he had a half-volley from outside the box saved, and swerved another shot around the wall which just whistled past the post. As Chelsea manager and Dutch superstar, Ruud Gullit, said afterwards on *Match Of The Day*: "Beckham was the only one in the first half that offered any real threat."

But his best game yet came in England's next World Cup qualifier, a 2—0 home victory over Georgia, courtesy of goals from Shearer and Sheringham, playing together for the first time since Euro 96.

"The confidence grows with every match," said Becks. "A lot is down to the manager, who encourages me all the time. He talks to me and passes on a lot of things on the training pitch. He is doing all he can to increase my confidence [and] I am beginning to feel part of the set-up."

It looks as though Gascoigne's days in the central midfield role for England will be over the moment Hoddle has the courage to play Beckham there in competitive matches and not just friendlies. He certainly looked more convincing playing in the middle in the exceptional 2—0 defeat of Italy, in Le Tournoi de France, in June (England's first victory against the Italians for 20 years), than he did stuck out on the right in the commendable 2—0 defeat of Poland a few days earlier.

Becks is confident he could do the job. "If the manager said that he wanted me to start influencing games, then I know I could live up to that responsibility. The position I play is down to him. I'd play anywhere, although I do prefer it in the middle of the midfield... If I could be half the player he was at international level, I would be happy."

Certainly, Beckham's development is about to become even more crucial as Manchester United face their first season for six years without Eric Cantona to guide them. Unpredictable to the last, Cantona had announced his retirement from football on May 18, news which completely overshadowed Chelsea's 2—0 victory over Middlesbrough in the FA Cup final at Wembley the day before.

In a short official statement, Cantona had said: "I've played professional football for 13 years, which is a long time. I now wish to do other things. I always planned to retire when I was at the top and at Manchester United I've reached the pinnacle of my career."

Fergie confessed he had tried everything to persuade Eric not to go, but refused to speculate on a possible successor. Paul Scholes has long been mentioned as an understudy for the Frenchman's free-ranging role. It was Juninho's name, however, that was on everybody's lips for days afterwards, but it was to be Spurs' and England's Teddy Sheringham whom Fergie would opt for to fill King Eric's boots.

One thing's for sure, as David May says, with Becks, Scholes, Butt, Giggs and the Nevilles in the side, "We can keep this up for the next five or six years."

On the charge: Success in the Champions' Cup remains United's major goal in the years ahead

And with the average age of the side just 23, things, as Tony Blair says, can only get better! Already favourites to win a fifth Premiership title in 1998, as Becks says: "The more you achieve, the more people expect of you. I know I have to maintain the standard I have set with United. I believe I will. All I want to do is play football, and when you boil it down, that is all I've ever wanted to do."

Latterly, it was revealed that the mighty AC Milan had come in with a bid of £15 million for Beckham. An astonishing figure for a young player still to reach his peak — until you consider that arch rivals Inter Milan were about to table an offer of nearly £50 million for Barcelona's 20-year-old Brazilian superstar Ronaldo.

Milan manager Arigo Sacchi had stated: "We are interested in David Beckham. He is one of the most exciting midfielders in Europe. Obviously Manchester United would not wish to sell him, but we believe every player has his price."Maybe. But the truth is you can't simply buy players like David Beckham. They have to want to go. And right now that's the last thing on his mind. Becks says his ambition in the short-term is to play for England in the World Cup in France. Long-term, he looks set to captain both Manchester United and England one day.

"I don't think I ever sit back and think, 'I wonder how things will turn out this time next year?'," he says. "Ideally, I want to be as successful as possible with Manchester United and continue to develop my career with England."

Far from ending here, the story of David Beckham has only just begun...